The Stand Up Poet.

Selected poems by Jack Hughes

Second Printing from September 2011

ISBN 978-1-4477-6640-7

Book Layout by Prague Spring Productions

Cover Design by Dubcek Designs

Back Cover Photograph by Grant David Read

Published by By The Wall Books

Printed by Lulu in the USA

Dedicated to my Grandparents; all of whom had a way with words, told great stories, inspired great stories and belonged to a generation which fought for everything we enjoy today.

Charlie; just thinking of you brings a smile.

Mum and Dad; for the jokes, songs, books and stories

Pat & Jim; for all those trips to museums and days out.

Acknowledgements

Thanks to the following

My editors, David Jackson-Smith and Lynn Adabayo for their continuing patience, indulgence and firmness on this project as with all others.

All the Freeway Poets, Louise and Mark and my students, who make going to work an enjoyable exercise.

The Daveys, Barbearys, Homers, Buckleys and Botts for all the good times; some of which are recounted in this anthology.

My colleagues in the funniest and wittiest staffroom this side of Fenn Street.

Contents

A Day At The Beach
The Right to an Education
This Is An Opportunity For You To Recognise
When You Got The Goblin Market
The Retardation of a Generation
Mind The Gap
Advice To A Teacher Doing Last Minute Cover
Sauberung
I Wasn't There
To A Bereaved Friend
Tribute To Gil Scott-Heron
Ticket to Ride

Introduction

In my last term of Primary school I gained two gold stars on the same day; the first was for a story about a heroin smuggling gang being thwarted by a trio of brave souls who were loosely based on myself and my two best mates. The second was for a poem about sharks called 'Red Blood, White Death'.

All the poems in this book were written between October 2010 and June 2011 and represent a taste of what my background in a perfectly normal dysfunctional family, my politics, the absurdities of the world around me and memories of time spent with good friends have influenced me to write.

This anthology contains free speech and may upset the politically correct classes; something for which I make no apology. However, I offer my sincerest apologies for the glaring omission of stories about heroin smugglers and poems about sharks.

Part One: Who Am I and Does It Matter? (Beware of The Personal Pronoun)

This Is Me

**When I'm up here on the stage,
or putting words on a page,
I try and speak honestly
when I tell you about me.**

**Though I'm from London
you'll never hear me chat
any Jafaican or use Mockney.**

**Not because I want to be taken
particularly seriously
but because when I wrote this
I was aged forty-three,
and I've spent most of my life
in a small town called Banbury.**

**So me, talking G would
just sound silly.**

**I've got working class routes
but live a middle class life;
semi-detached house, one son
and an ex-wife.**

**I listen to NWA and KRS1
but just 'cos they rap about
gangsters doesn't mean
I wannabe one.**

**I've never carried a knife,
never been in fear of my life,
I know people who could get
me a gun, but don't envisage
a situation where I'd ever
need one.**

**Despite screwing up my
secondary education and
leaving school with an O level
count of one more than none
I managed to stage a revolution
centred around my brain
and now have more letters
following than I've got in my name.**

**Whether it's with pen and paper,
a microphone or chalk and slate
what gives me the confidence
to articulate my thoughts and ideas
for other peoples' eyes and ears
is that I hold no fears
about being proved wrong or
losing a debate because
listening to others helps me to
formulate my own thoughts and
to recognise there is no such thing
as being totally self-taught
and that the biggest prize
is talking with someone
who is more wise.**

**Because when you give that respect
you are learning to respect yourself
and what could be better for your
well being and your mental wealth?**

**So I'll conclude with a Latin homily;
cogito ergo sum,
which allows me to think freely
and use words powerfully
and to honestly be me.**

A Banbury Childhood

**Down by the canal,
Now the location of
The new bus station,
Stood a former textile factory.
Where I found a loomwieght
Which in my imagination
Was a Nazi bomb
But in reality was a souvenir,
A piece of history
From an industry,
A working building
Semi-demolished because of
Recession? Relocation?
That heavy remnant of
A working moment became an
Ornament in my childhood home.
A reminiscence and reminder
Of my right to roam
Around the town where I grew up.
Where my imagination meant
That every industrial building
That skirted the Cut had to be
Stormed and taken.**

**The long gone cantilever
Bridge had to be held at all costs
And the weir over the River Cherwell
Was the host to many a daring
Commando raid on a Saturday,
After a morning spent in the Wimpy
Eating burgers, chips and chocolate milkshakes.**

The bridge over the river
Into Spiceball Park was
Attacked on many occasions.
Dynamited, held, defended to
The death...depending on who played
A goodie or a baddie.
Adults? What were they?
They didn't exist in my Saturdays.

And on weekday evenings
After school, playing football
In 'The Field' behind the Art College
Up Mewburn Road. Where the
Big kids would dominate the game
And we would do the same when
We became big as well.
'The Field', another place
Where we would face
Imaginary enemies from the
Master race and we would die
A thousand heroic deaths doing
In play what our grand-dads had done
For real in their day.
Names and faces from those days
Are seared like a welcome scar
On my brain. A lesion that gives
Legion to a gang of boys who chased
And played, got hurt and got up
Bruised and grazed. I remember cut heads
And broken bones, falling out of trees
And going home crying, not defying
The pain. But, later returning to the
Game stitched up and showing off
A limb in plaster, which, with the

Right artwork could become a ray gun
Or atom blaster.

With some of those names
I still remain in contact to
This day, despite having
Moved away. Foundations of
Stone laid back in those days
When we played with toy guns and
Plastic hand grenades, where no
Part of town had any barricades
To us because we just did what we
Did and never questioned that it was
Fun to be a kid.

In the People's Park and the
Outdoor pool we played.
Or we just stayed on the estate
And went round each other's houses
Not even contemplating that one day
We would grow up and our games would
Change and we would reject what we
Did as kids as being from another age.
Because, back then, all that growing up
And boring stuff seemed such a long way
away

An Odyssey With Homer

**We were both unprepared
when we went
off with rucksacks and a
small tent. Clinging to a rudimentary
grasp of French,
We chatted up that girl on the ferry
and her Mum drove us around Calais
to a camp site in
the town. Those Algerian kids
came over and helped us to
get set and we paid them
in cigarettes. We left the next day,
early enough so as not to pay and got on
the train to Paris. That women gave
us a bag of oranges and we continued to escape
that which made us feel trapped. A
relationship gone wrong and the cloying
feeling of unemployment.
I recall the night
we saw the sites of Florence.
Or Firenze as we said,
because in our heads
we were travelers, not tourists,
not Brits on the piss.
As we drunk our cheap wine
comme campesi
and things got hazy
with that girl from South Africa we
lost the next day.
We met those two New York yanks
and chatted about Woody Allen,
and Jazz with those girls from LA.
We met Aussies, Kiwis, Glaswegians and Canadians
in Nice, where I was mugged,
and in Milan where we laughed in the cathedral**

and had to run out as we got evil
looks from men in long black cloaks.
Agropoli, southern Italy
was for me the best
bit of the trip. Where we
were skint but never
hungry as strangers came to us in
the street and asked to eat
with them in their houses.
And we joined that family
in that bar by the beach
because they and their kids
couldn't eat all the pizza
that came in big square boxes
that were as big as the tables
we were sat at.

Up and down the boot of
Italy, across to Corfu on a
ferry where we met up with
Jay and Sean and slept in an orange grove.
Finding out that oranges are actually green.
I slept outside on a mat, you in the tent
as we spent our time trying to
find ourselves. And when we did
we went home via Rome and
walked around the coliseum
with that American girl just bummin' around
her gap year who was scornful
about her compatriots who stayed stateside
believing Europe was 'at war' with Libya.
Our final train trip on the mainland,
20 hours from Rome to Calais, 16
spent sleeping, missing Switzerland
completely, unshaven and smelly,
back on a ferry to Dover, our journey nearly
done. On our first English train

we heard the welcome home refrain
that the wrong kind of rain would
delay our triumphant reappearance
in our local pub. Not one delayed journey
in a month in France, Greece and Italy.

We got back to no jobs and a Government Tory,
Our Odyssey was over, but we'd made
our own history and created a story
that would get bigger with every telling,
and 20 odd years later our horizons are
still broader from that eye opener of a sojourn,
that allowed us, for a time
to forget what we'd escaped from.

Bitter Sweet

Is it perhaps a little unhealthy
To get nostalgic about chocolate
Bars like Topic or Golden Cup
Or Swisskit, you know, the one
With the avalanche and the bloke
Who'll risk it?

Is it possibly a little pathetic
To be transported back to childhood
Via the memories of coco-pops,
Golden Nuggets and Bourbon biscuits?

Should I be at least a little concerned
That the taste of such unhealthy snacks
Are forever burned into my psyche? Along
With Kia-Ora, Panda Pops, Um Bongo,
Chewits, Refreshers, Texan Bars and Toffifee.

Am I perhaps missing a trick?
Could it be that all those Wagon Wheels
And Wine Gums round my Nan's are
The reason I'm now Diabetic?
All those sugar dummies, sugar mice
Cakes that were naughty but nice,
Cola bottles, Cola Cubes, KP Discos,
Outer Spacers, Flying Saucers, Frazzles
And Froobs.

So now I have to hold firm,
Be strong and like a Grange Hill kid,
Just say no to sugary sweet things
That could cause me woe.

However, just the other day,
I saw a Walnut Whip and I couldn't
Resist. My resolve started to sway,
I gave in and as I ate it I thought
To myself, fuck it...who needs ten toes anyway?

Carpe Diem

Do I have to seize the day?
Can't I just go for a coffee,
Read a book, see a film,
Meet some mates for a
Couple of beers and then
Go home and watch the telly?
I'll Carpe Diem tomorrow,
I've got nothing else on.

The First Day At College

Standing around,
Holding our ground.
Smoking, chatting,
LOUD.
Marking territory,'
The uncertainty of youthful individualism,
Seeking the safety of a group.
Standing out, fitting in.
Standing around.

A Comment On Music

On the telly, the C list celebrity
will say it was all about
Spandau Ballet and Duran Duran.
Bollocks, they were crap

But I did like Japan & OMD and
The Bunnymen and Bowie and
His weird mate from San Francisco
Called Klaus Nomi

And that sexy French woman called Ronnie
Grace Jones with beats laid down
By Sly and Robbie
A 12" by Paul Hardcastle

Entitled Guilty, memories of Motown
and Tighten Up albums at
Mum and Dad's parties.
Never Too Much,

Glow Of Love and Searching
Put me on a soul boy tip.
Caister, Southport and Prestatyn.
All – Dayers, All Nighters,

What a laugh, buy the records,
get some 1200s, be a DJ.
But I move forward too fast.
What about when

Morrissey met Marr?
Still my favourites,
even my son
Loves The Smiths;

**Stephen's words, Johhny's riffs.
No Smash Hits for me
When I was at school,
That would've been too uncool.**

**Oily fingers from reading
The NME, Sounds and one about
Makers of melody. Then came the Face,
glossy pictures of Kraftwerk and Sade.**

**Blues and Soul read like a Bible,
Sometimes Echoes,
When I was able to find it.
The Clash and Ian Dury told us to pogo on a Nazi.**

**For Ian that can't have been easy!
The Beastie Boys told us
To Fight For The Right
To Party. Run, Jay and**

**Darrell Mac, were Raisin' Hell.
Chuck D raised our level of wisdom
And awareness as did KRS1 with his
Philosophy. Rightful heirs**

**To The Last Poets and
Gil Scott Heron, the revolution, televised
Or not, was their spoken word.
No confusion. Johnny Cash in**

**San Quentin, Hurt, Walking The
Line. His American Gypsy life.
Solomon Burke called country
The White Man's Blues, listen**

To Cash and you'll know that
too. Then listen to Muddy Waters
and Howlin' Wolf and their blues
And let it take you to English boys;

The Kinks and The Who.
Don't worry, you can download that
Too. But this poem isn't about musical advice,
Rather it's a device to allow me

To reminisce about Terry Callier,
Ordinary Joe, Don't Want To See Myself
Without You. Roy Ayers and
Frankie Beverley and Maze singing songs about

Everybody loving Sunshine And Rain. Losing
My Religion, Insane In The Brain, Rebel
Without A Pause; all these tunes give
Me cause to reflect on the influence

In my life of playing music, from time
when I used to stack 7" singles on
My Dad's record player. One record
Stops, kerchunk, the next one drops.

My Christmas present music
centre, with turntable, radio
And Dolby sound. Whatever that
Was. To my 1200s, my CD Player,

My MP3. And when I can I pass
On those tunes because it was
Never all about Fucking Spandau
Ballet or Poxy Duran Duran. Not

When great bands like The Stone Roses,
Sly and The Family Stone
and Joy Division were at hand. Troubadors
With guitars, Bob Dylan, Richie Havens,

Bobby Womack, all sure to
Make you tap your feet,
sing along, learn their words
you claim as yours. Songs

That get you through the
Five days until The Weekend Comes,
When you'll have some fun. Fred Wesley
Telling us to roll back the carpet,

Move the chairs, We're Gonna Have
A House Party. When I wrote this
I did insist to myself
this wouldn't just be a list

Of my favourite singers and bands
Maybe I failed in that but just
understand Mr Ex Blue Peter
Presenting C List Celebrity,

It was always more than
Duran Duran and Spandau
Ballet. Now I will finish
With a confession. I did

Own a copy of Duran's first
LP. The one with Planet Earth
And Girls on Film. But I never
Owned anything by those Essex

Boys, Spandau Ballet and
That Much Is True. Except that one
They did with Beggar and Co.
That one was good.

Part Two: Never Mind the Politics (It's all bollocks)

When Tony Benn Didn't Come Round For Tea

I wanted to live in a house
Where left-wing intellectuals came round
And sat down at my oak kitchen table
To discuss Marx and Hegel.
We'd plot how apartheid would fall
And have well constructed but
Heated debates about the Berlin Wall
Our French cigarettes would burn away,
Half smoked and forgotten
In an ashtray bearing the insignia of the NUM.
A gift from when I performed my poetry
At a miners' benefit gig;
Coming on between the alternative comedian from Liverpool
And the left wing, maverick, Labour MP.
At my table would be Tony Benn,
A Chilean Trades Unionist and Red Ken.
And as we discussed the fate
Of The Sandinistas, picking at
Yugoslavian goats milk cheese on our plates,
My mind would wander and I
Would ponder on how I am
Holding my own
With these left-wing intellectuals,
Who aren't sitting in my home.

Who Runs Britain?

Who runs Britain
When the power's off?
When the power's off
Who's at the helm?
Who runs Britain
When the coal runs out?
When the coal runs out
Who strikes up the orchestra?
Who runs Britain
When the public eat by candlelight?
When the public eats by candlelight
Who sets the tempo?
Who runs Britain
When there's a three day week?
When there's a three day week
Who skippers the boat?
Who runs Britain?
If you have to ask the question
Then it's not you.

The Hatfield Anti-Nazi League

Heavy set white blokes, Ben Shermans, short hair,
Walking with the Union Jack carrying
Racists. Were they shocked when you and your
mates landed punches in their Nazi faces?

You were the football supporters, the soul
Crew white boys from the estates and the
Factories who didn't use words like wog,
Paki or yids. But they thought you did. So you

Infiltrated and put in the boot and
You killed off the NF at their zenith.
When words weren't enough you used your strengths
of righteous violence for a fight that was right.

One by one they didn't come back, frightened
Off by the attack from those who looked like
Them and spoke like them but who thought with an
Intelligence and wit when they fought the

The mental corruption of an idea
Based on ignorance and hate that had
No place in this United Kingdom of
Working class heroes from Cable Street to

Lewisham,Southall, Cricklewood and Kilburn.
Leeds, Manchester, Sheffield, Luton, Watford,
Orgreave, Peterloo, Brixton, Tottenham,
Handsworth, Glasgow, Cardiff and Bradford.

Wherever the fascists went you were there
The Hatfield Anti-Nazi League. The knights
Of a Britain that saw no place for dumb
Blind ignorance of a colour based master race.

No More Giants?

Where are the giants?
The Foots, the Benns and the Castles.
They've been replaced by ideologically
Uncertain women & men;
Ubergeeks & supernerds
Who seem to spend their time
Second guessing and placating
Hypocritical and self-serving
Media barons.

Where are the giants?
MPs who had jobs and trades.
They've been replaced by party
Approved apparatchiks and SPADS.
PPE Grads from a narrow elite
That have led socialism to a
Dishonourable defeat instead
Of flying the red flag and closing
The gap between the have mores
And don't haves.

Where are the giants?
Once proud to stand alongside the unions,
They've been replaced by those happy to
Keep Tory employment legislation.
Designed to keep down the working
Men and women and destroy the skills
And expertise that once characterised
A 'you are what you do' instead of
A 'you are what you own' nation.

Where are the giants?
I know you're out there somewhere.

Mugging St Francis of Assisi

I started Secondary School in September 1978
And we had one text book each.
On our return from the Summer
In September 1979
We had one book between five.
Because in May of that year
Britain was delivered from discord
And was brought harmony,
How lucky were we?

The Iron Lady-Rust In Peace

In anticipation of the eventual demise of Thatcher,
My notification of my contempt for the milk snatcher,
is a T-Shirt designed for just this event.

On it is a picture of her grave.
Above that the word, writ large, DANCEFLOOR.
For it is my intention to rave
on that metaphorical plot of land.
My feet dancing to the repetitive beats
she tried to ban.

Locked out of heaven, she will be in purgatory
for an eternal time, reflecting on her callous decisions
to close down mines, the steelworks, the shipyards
and all the places that gave working men their
identities and allowed them to hold high
their faces.

In my mind I see her at the gates of hell,
arguing with the Devil who will yell
'go away, you can't come in'.
And she will demand 'why not, I
did your work in earnest?
The Devil will shake his horned head and shout,
'Because you're not closing down MY furnace'.

Proverbial Cuts 2010-11

Due to the recent cuts,
the Con-Dem coalition
has made these revisions
to the following proverbs.

The light at the end of
the tunnel will now be
switched off.

The linings of clouds will
now be coloured bronze.

The exchange rate for birds
in the hand will now be
worth one and a half in the bush.

And if you feel flush
and are inclined to invest
in a stitch in time then
be aware it will no longer
be worth nine.

An Essay on The Modern Day Reality of Social Mobility

Social Mobility seems such an empty phrase in this era of public school and Old Etonian hegemony and the return to the days of toffs running the country.

Has Britain gone back to the 1940s and 50s when policy was spawned on the grouse moors by men whose opinions were formed in their upbringing by nannies?

From the mid sixties to the middle 90s there was an all too brief moment of egality when the sons and daughters of carpenters, jugglers and grocers ran our country.

In Wilson, Heath, Callaghan, Major and yes, even Thatcher, whatever their political shade, these people had made their own way without the benefit of the colours and stripes of an old school tie to smooth their way up the greasy pole. Now, however, meritocracy is nothing more than a fallacy when Boris, George and David, 'call me Dave' are old pals from their Bullingdon days, and deputy Nick is another elitist who played the floppy fringed trick to make his way up the lubricated stick.

Where is the credibility in the claim 'we're all in this together' when they all come from nests feathered by landowning and titled ancestors.

This isn't a call for posh boys to be excluded; that would just be class war stupid and not a little prejudiced, after all it was an Old Harrovian who led Britain in the fight against Nazis and Fascists and a Haileybury old boy who created the NHS.

But, in modern Britain, what is the reality of those born into poverty or educated in the stultifying mediocrity of a system designed to hit targets rather than educate with depth and quality?

Exclusion from power, from Oxbridge universities, exclusion from those positions in the economy where there is the influence of the wealthy. Exclusion based on a misfortune of progeny.

A new reality where in the second decade of the 21st century the ceiling of glass has been replaced by one made from the mud and the grass of the playing fields of Eton.

A reality that once again must be beaten and power based on an accident of birth must be reversed so that once and for all opportunity for all is not just an empty slogan but a living breathing norm based on skills and intelligence and not the singing of the old school song.

Part Three: Considered Observations on Hypocrisy, Absurdity and The Human Condition.

(He's been at The Guardian again)

A Penny To Watch The Freaks

In the 18th century
The great and the good could pay one penny
To stare into Bedlam's cells
And view the freak show.
In a perverted twist of equality,
Every month it was free,
For the poor to see,
If they went on the first Tuesday.
Now, let us think about
the nature of that hypocrisy
in the caring and enlightened 21st Century.
Where, if you watch Jeremy Kyle
on the tele, no matter how ironically,
he's a cunt,
But then you're no better than he.

A Note on A Penny To Watch The Freaks:

I wrote this poem after hearing that my former English lecturer, Nell Leyshon, was to be the first female playwright to be performed at The Globe since its opening in 1599.

On reading that her play was set in the hospital from where we get the word bedlam, I read up on its history. It was as a result of this research that I wrote 'A Penny To Watch The Freaks'. I would like to thank Nell for playing a big part in my love of literature and writing.

To anyone who does watch Jeremy Kyle and is offended by my poem, good, that was my intention.

Apochryphal of Nonsense

**Despite constant warnings
I've yet to meet anyone whose
Arm has been broken by a swan.
Similarly, I don't know of anyone
Who's died from swallowing chewing gum.**

**Have you ever met a person
Who, after a change in the wind's direction,
Has found themselves in a situation
Where their reflection is fixed
In a grotesque contortion?**

**Many times I've gone swimming
After a meal and yet
I'm still here to tell the tale,
And without fail I received
Christmas presents as a kid,
In spite of the naughty things I did.**

**I have a recently diagnosed
Lactose intolerant friend
Whose disappointment is utter,
Because in her younger years
A specifically placed yellow flower
Indicated that she did indeed
Love butter.**

**No matter how hungry,
My eyes are never bigger than my belly
And they've never gone square
After hours of watching the tele.**

I've no idea what tricks
Triple scoring footballers do with a hat,
And I'm not convinced that my luck
Will be affected no matter
On which path I encounter a black cat.

I'm confident that languages
Other than my own
Don't all sound Greek.
I've looked on maps
And I'm yet to find a river
Named Shit Creek or a sea
With Straits labelled Dire.

And despite hearing politicians
Speak on numerous occasions
I've never seen pants on fire.

C2 Toilet Paper

**I feel like my head's going to explode
like a cliche all over a page.
You adverberlise your cries of outrage
and high moral indignation
to a faction of the nation
that wants to join you in
crucifying the perpetrators
of every sexual sin, at the same
time as their hands are in their
flies , caressing themselves
as they read half lies about
3rd rate mime acts and
fantasize about wham bam
with sexy Sam, just 16 years
old, from East Ham, smiling on
the 3rd page, two pages before the outraged
comments of the
'tell it like it is',
'man in the street',
'man of the people',
who wants you to despise and victimise
anyone who denies
his narrowed mind, closed eyes
view of the world.
And the editor of this 'solar',
or 'stellar' or maybe 'reflective'
rag will blag a seat at the top table,
with his media tycoon boss
just because of the perception
that they are able to deliver,
into the hands of politicians
and purveyors of X-Factored scams,
the votes and the cash of the families
of drivers of colour deficient vans.**

The Unwitting Comedian

Skinny, spotty, track-suited & white; mouth open
And out comes shite spoken in a voice made up
Of cod cliché and stereotype.
An attempt to sound vaguely London and Caribbean
But actually sounding like an impression from a
1970's racist comedian. Trying to sound urban and
Street but actually only succeeding in reminding
The world of that wanker, Jim Davidson.
A man , who spread his lowest common denominator
'hilarity' via his version of a Jamaican Amos and
Andy that he 'oh so ironically' named Chalky,
because he was that fucking funny.
So white boy you don't sound 'G', you don't sound
'down wit dat', you just sound like a stupid twat.
Find your own identity.

Bullshit For Dummies

Like Mecutio I want to wish a pox;
On the houses of those who use
The asinine phrase 'think outside the box'.

I would love to see a ship torpedoed
And sinking, full of those idiots
Who talk about 'Blue sky thinking'.

In addition it should be perfectly legal
To bury somebody up to their neck
And leave them for the vultures
If they ever suggest 'solution cultures'.

Workshop is a noun,
And the name given to where
Light engineering takes place.
Anyone who uses it as a verb
Deserves a smack in the face.
'Hi, let's workshop this through'.
No, you come here so I can introduce
You to a long heeled lady's shoe.

'There's no I in team'.
What does that actually mean?
There's no Zed in horse either
And furthermore no H in Zebra.
Oh, look Geoff from marketing,
Guess what, there's no X in abracadabra.

Who is to blame for the peddling
Of this meaningless tosh?
Those who sell it or the Emperors
who buy into this candy floss?

One good thing I suppose
Is that whoever uses this useless prose,
Whether politicians, middle managers or bankers,
At least they're identifying themselves
For what they are;
Over-employed wankers.

Language and Lexis are such powerful tools
Don't be taken in by the Orwellian newspeak
Of shallow fools. I issue a clarion call
To all people of gorm, intelligence and wit;
Resist the perfidious spread of this
Meaningless verbal shit.

Because we all have the choice
To use the language of Shakespeare,
Dryden and Pope. Billy Bragg, Irvine Welsh,
Becket, Yeats, Duffy and Wendy Cope.

Furthermore, we're Geordies, Mackems,
Cockneys, Wurzels, Scousers and Brummies.
So, don't insult us with language
Taken from 'Bullshit For Dummies'.

Dividing Assets

He went home and
Confessed his infidelity.
She seemed to take it
Quite calmly.
So they went to bed
and she said, 'I still
Want you, shall I do
That thing you like me
To do'?
'Yes' he replied eagerly and without pause.
And now, whenever he goes
To the gents, he feels the need
To explain he lost half of
Everything in the divorce.

I Am The DJ

Everyone mingles while I play 12 inch singles
And get nice and drunk as I slam on
Acid House, Hip-Hop, Breakbeats and Funk.
On the turntables I hold sway
Over the tunes I select and choose
As you all dance and drink your booze.

When I'm on the vinyl slates
I can make you hit the floor
Like someone settling a score
And you throw shapes, bust moves,
Lose yourself in the grooves.
And you get higher and higher
And sing like your part of a gospel choir.

And the next day on a comedown
And/or hangover, with your knees aching
And ankles on fire you'll tell yourself
It's time to stop the rave and then you'll
Meet me again and you'll think
'Nah, I'll stop dancing when I'm in my grave'.
I am the DJ

I Don't Believe In Fairies

The time came when I had to resist
the idea that Father Christmas
really did exist. I was aged 9,
but it was fine, I'd known for some time
that it was Mum and Dad who put
presents under the tree, not made
by elves, but bought by Nans,
Grandads, Uncles and Aunties
and not the result of a visit by
a fat bloke who knew whether
I'd been nice or naughty.
Despite having already sussed
the mythology of the tooth fairy,
I took a position contrary
to that knowledge; in order to
keep open the milk tooth
futures market that would net
the price of a Marvel comic.
With Santa and the Tooth Fairy
thoroughly dismissed to the list
of concepts and creatures such
as Leprechauns and Unicorns I
grew up and started to wonder
which other childhood stories
should be shod. I began to question
the existence of God. I have wrestled
with this conundrum for many years
and for answers started to read
Aquinus, Marx and Socrates.
Was I wrong to doubt the reality of
a great creator, the Universe's instigator?
A being who, if so inclined, might
punish my lack of belief with a well

aimed smite. The more I enquired
the more I saw the whole idea of
religion as preposterous and to follow
Voltaire's thinking, an excuse to
commit the atrocious. I discussed
and debated with Priests, Rabbis
and Imams. I read the Bible, the Torah
and the Holy Qu'ran. A preacher told
me that Jesus was his teacher and
his life had meaning because of the
Holy Trinity. I concluded that it was
the same for me but that my trinity
was art and science and philosophy
not Espirito Sanctum, Filius et Padre.
I understood religion as the catalyst for
war and oppression and couldn't
see what good it brought to
me and to you. I related this
to a former Rabbi, now a
secular Jew and he made me
understand that conflicts like
that of Israel and Palestine
was about control of land and
not to dismiss religion out
of hand. He set me a test,
a quest if you will, to take my trinity
of art, science and philosophy and
add to it identity and comedy and
to look and analyse them as
if the concept of God and gods had
never been. So I did and I saw
wonderful things; statues, buildings,
paintings, great writings. Stories,
legends and myths. Scheherazade,
Salome, Paradise Lost and Regained.
cathedrals, the Blue Mosque, the
Temple at Amritsar. Places where

people come to be as one, even
if just for a Friday, a Sabbath,
to meet, to talk, to sing great
songs. Choirs singing praises
that make the hairs on your
arms stand to attention and
quicken your heart. Mozart,
Handel, Titian, Caravaggio;
inspired to create art because
of a belief in a creator. But
what about humour? I had
been told to test the effects of
religion on the work of clowns
and jesters and purveyors of
fun. This test, the hardest part
of my quest, was finally put
to rest when on a sign that
said Jesus Saves, someone had
added, 'But Moses Invests'. So
now I stand secular and atheist,
and on the existence of God with
Dawkins and Hawkins. But Like
Marx, I understand that a world
where religion were banned
would not be a better place
but something quite bland.
Bless you, Shalom, Salaam.

I'm A Role Model

My old flat,
A den of iniquity,
Was a classic example of
A place of total equality;
Bring a case of Becks
And some vinyl for the decks
And the door was open
To all in the vicinity.

Now a million years on
My son seems to have
The same open door philosophy.
But as he's only a kid,
I've banned the booze completely and
I'm a parent who enforces that strictly.

So I'll supply the Sunny Delight
As my son and his mates
Slaughter each other on the X-Box 360.

Insomnia

When sleep doesn't come
And you lie awake listening
To every rattle and hum
As your flat has
A conversation with itself.
Do you, in the gloom,
Allow your eyes to wander around
Your tomb of a room
Taking stock of books on the shelf?
Praying that the act of reading
In bed will produce the desired result
Of a journey to the land of nod?
Instead of the purgatorial
Limbo of tossing and turning
under your duvet, contemplating
whether to start a sub mattress
search for a small green pea
lost from its pod.
Do you stare at the haphazard
Arrangement of Pants and socks
Patterning the floor
Evidence of an aim
Unsure in your
Olympiad ritual
Of throwing the day's
Underclothes in the basket
And failing to score.
Do you notice every detail
Of the shadows cast on the wall
From the curtain filtered

Sodium of the inconveniently sited
Street lamp just outside your
Bedroom window.
When, despite your need to sleep,
Will your mind continue to roam
Over the events of the day just gone
And the one yet to come,
When you'd happily exchange a kidney
Or any other vital organ
Just for the chance to
Be happily snoring
Instead of existing in the half world
Of too tired to be awake.
Where even the promise of a few hours kip,
a simple doze or 40 winks
would encourage you to
find a crossroads and do a deal
with the devil himself.

Do you make the mistake that is fatal
Of watching the clock that is digital
Willing the night to end and marveling at
How long a minute really is.
Or do you do as I do
And fantasise as in your mind's eye
You run through a rewritten life and
Construct a fable where you
Score winning world cup goals,
Record seminal soul LPs
With the Memphis Horns
At Muscle Shoals,
Have the ability to fly or
Travel through time,
Speak seven languages, read other peoples'

Minds and get away with a masterplan for
Robbing a bank.
Or do you just think bollocks to
This and pass the
Time by having a wank?

Keys and Coins

Keys and coins rattling and beating
A tattoo to mark a step by step retreat
Away from the synthetic fun of the
Wide-screened bars.

All notes gone, no cash for cab
Or kebab, just glad of that not
Quite empty pack of fags that
Has survived the night.

Home, where the Toast is and Marmite
And tea and biscuits and a laptop and
Facebook, where you can alert the world
To your inebriation by posting from
Youtube, old classic tunes to provoke a
Reaction.

And so, when all that is left on the TV
Is home shopping and repeats for the deaf,
It is time for bed. Like a man dancing with
Himself, getting undressed is symbolised
And signified by the cymbal crash of keys
And coins as they rain from pocket to floor.

Life's A Drag

I like going to the pub with my mates
And talking shit and telling lies.
I used to love boxing on the tele
'Til it all went on Sky.
I loved playing Rugby and when on
The pitch it was not unusual
To get into a ruck and throw a
Few fists. Then, in true blokey fashion,
At the whistle we'd all shake hands,
Go to the bar and get pissed.

But I have a secret which I must confess;
I have a real yearning to wear a dress.
Now, please note, this isn't an admission
Of a conversion to transvestism.
No, my desire is linked to another scene;
The truth is that for one night only,
I long to be a drag queen.

I want an all over wax and a fitted gown.
And make acerbic and catty
remarks into a microphone.
When I come on stage I want
To vamp and prance and use
Double entendres as I thank
The audience for the warm hand
On my entrance.

I want to murder Bette Midler
And belt out Judy Garland
And sing that song secretaries on
Hen nights sing about being petrified,
Throwing away the key and surviving.

And when it's all over
And I've milked the applause
I'll get a taxi home and when
Indoors I'll drop My Donna Karin,
Size 24, onto my living room floor.
And remove from my head my
Blonde fake thatch, turn on
The TV and watch Deadliest Catch.
Then, swigging from a can of lager,
I'll give my balls a bloody good scratch.

Living In The Moment Too Soon

Don't tell me to live in the moment
When I'm still catching up with my past.
It's pointless to live in the moment
When hopes and fears are inevitably
Influenced by those done and finished years.

Logic states you can't get those years back
But logic doesn't stop that head attack
That all the time nags and chats at the back
Of your mind; 'til you find yourself lost in a self-
absorbed
Nostalgia of an 'if I could do it all again' neuralgia.

Is trying to change a past nothing more than
A J. Arthur? A self-indulgent onanistic exercise
That feels good but still leaves the same mess to
Clean up after. Or can it catapult an idea of a
Positive future where your mistakes
Become both mentor and tutor?

Where you strive to reach a state of equilibrium,
A balance between experience and opportunity
And the recognition that 'you are who you are' also
Means you can be who you want to be.
Be your own life coach, your own Angelo Dundee,
Drop mind bombs as powerful as the fists of
Muhammed Ali.

Regain your past, own your history.
Inform your future, anticipate its mystery.
Treat the present as both prologue and epilogue
That happen simultaneously, let the moment pass
And add the experience to your itinerary. Marcel
Proust wrote that in 14 volumes of ingenuity.

I'm not going to live in the moment;
I'm living my life in its entirety.

The TV Warm Up Man

The TV warm up man takes the stage
And fiddling with the mic takes
It from its stand.
Then, looking at the audience,
He plants on his face a smile,
Broad and toothy, which
Could grace any photograph
Taken at a friend's wedding,
Or composed on the silver
Medal position of a podium.

He interacts with the crowd
In order to goad them into
A feeling of conviviality,
Humour and jollity.
Moving around the stage,
He builds a rapport by making
Post modern and ironic observations
About the everyday machinations
Of day to day life.

Like how he only pays a tenner for a haircut,
Which is eight times cheaper than
It costs his wife.
'What's that all about'?
He asks after every quip.
He asks the audience the same
Question whether he's making
Comments on generic back seat
Fumblings on a long ago school trip
Or the middle class angst of

When to leave a tip.
'What's that all about'?
Again he asks, and he asks, and he asks after a well thought out spout about how you never see Spangles any more or anyone under 60
Carrying a tartan flask.

'What's that all about'?
The question never wears thin,
As he involves the audience
And cajoles them to join in.

'What's that all about'?
He shouts, with a look
Of mock incredulity on his face
After every joke about hoodies,
Celebrities and politicians'
Sexual traits.
'What's that all about'?
As he jokes about Cameron and Clegg
And how they lie and how Gordon
Brown is Scottish and has only one
Eye.

And when his time is up
And his job is done,
When the crowd's warmed up
And the audience is cheering as one
He announces 'I've been the warm up man,
Goodnight, thank you and enjoy the show'.
It's time for him to go, his gig is over
And that is that, then Jimmy Carr,
That Welsh bloke from Gavin and Stacey
And Lee Mack come on to record an

Episode of 8 out of 10 cats.
And the warm up man?
In his dressing room he is sat.
Contemplating what jokes to do,
When tomorrow night he does it all again
And warms up for 'Have I got News For you'.

Goodnight, I've been the warm up man,
Thank You!

The Wonder

Was it there or was it imagined?
That look, that feeling.

Did I see it, did you send it?
That vibe, that signal.

In this game, this ancient game that is as old as life and not just for man,
We can't always use words.
We use looks and signs and signals and smiles,
Our eyes and mouths and lips and cheeks
Widen and redden.
And our thoughts we wish to transmit
Because words may break this spell of magic uncertainty.

You say it first, you say it first,
Tell me you're part of the same ritual.
That same confusing ritual of sex and chemistry and feelings.
And nervous anticipation that entrances and enchants and elates
And mystifies all but the most cold of hearts.

Was it there or was it imagined?

The Quarry Pond At Hengistbury Head

**A catkin, the sole survivor of
a harvest of the reeds, stands
sentinel over the breeze dappled,
shifting surface of the pond.**

**Coloured the dark green of
the bank, oily black in the
gorse given shade and silver
tipped ripples where touched
by the sun.**

**A child's distant shout
and a bird's call mingle
with a dog's bark.**

**Footsteps on the path
behind warn of a break
in my solitude. Two red
cheeked boys run past;
acting out a war scene. Parents
half-heartedly call out,
'Not too far' then resume
their conversation.
And then, quiet again,
only the wind whispering
to the water, the bird calls
marking territory and place.
It again becomes my space.**

**Until some fucking kid goes past on a
skateboard.**

A Day At The Beach

Like dual windmills without synchronicity
Or symmetry, the kayakers paddle laterally
Across the view enjoyed by consumers
Of ice cream cornets and novels about
Working class northern lasses who live
In hovels, or young American
Lawyers fighting lost causes.

A game of football erupts between
Colombian language students and
A group of short haired, tattooed
Lads on a stag. The two styles of
The beautiful game apparent even
On sand. The jokes, the laughter
The cheers and jeers the same for
Both sides.

Bodies of every morphology compete
With the scenery of the Purbeck Hills
To the south-west. A man in a vest
Drinks beer and gives his kids money
To go on the pier, forgetting the usual
Paranoia and fear of letting the young
Out of sight.

**A family of Sikhs recreate Bhaji On
The Beach as they open a treasure
Trove of food once seen as exotic, but
Now, mundane and familiar to all. Hassids,
In long black coats organise a corral of
Sunbeds and deckchairs. Felt hats and
Yamulkah showing only the hair
Of their earlocks.**

**Paddlers, bathers, swimmers and
Sun worshippers, all gathered to divest
Themselves of worries, work and clothes.
The preservation of modesty utmost in
The minds of those who get changed
By dancing the beach towel Tango.**

**Hangovers are nursed, 'that last pint'
Cursed, stomachs are pulled in, breasts
Are showing, skin burning or tanning.
Bronze made deeper, a child's shriek
Of delight wakens a momentarily confused
sleeper.
A family of the socially unaware shout
And swear at their progeny in an attempt
To create an impression of parenting.**

**A grand scale project of civil engineering
Is undertaken by a family firm of Uncles
And Nephews and Sons and Cousins and
Dads, equipped with only buckets and spades
And imagination. A foreshadowing of what
Is to come when the tide comes in and the
Sun goes down.**

**For this day, spent in the UV rays and the
Saline of the bay will come to an end, marked
By holes dug in the sand, discarded frisbees,
Forgotten flip-flops and the sight of deckies
Dismantling striped, canvas chairs ready for
Herding away. Litter pickers march across
The sand, grabbers and black bags in hand as
They rush to finish; eager to hit the town all
Washed and brushed and groomed and combed.**

**And tomorrow? Tomorrow all this will
Start again, weather permitting.**

Part Four: The Many Faces of Education

The Human Rights Act 1998
Part II
Article 2
The right to an education.

In this classroom,
You have the right to make mistakes.
But you also have the responsibility to learn from your mistakes.
You have the right to freedom of expression.
But you also have the responsibility to express yourself effectively.
You have the right to freedom of thought.
But you also have the responsibility to read widely and ensure those thoughts are informed.
You have the right to free speech.
But you also have the responsibility to accept you may be challenged and may have to hear and listen to an opposing opinion.
But the main responsibility you have is to understand that this is an opportunity for you to recognise.

<u>This Is An Opportunity For You To Recognise.</u>

When you do less than your best
I am less than impressed
I don't care about your grade
That's for the number crunchers
The league table munchers
This is an opportunity for you to recognise

To parade your talent
Your thoughts and expression
In words, in writing,
In language, and with confidence
To tell your story whatever it is
In a forum where speech is free,
Don't waste it, use it
Find out who you are
Shout it and be it.
This is an opportunity for you to recognise

You have a pen and paper and a voice
Don't falter in the mistaken idea
That your opinions don't matter
Or that no one will want to hear
Your words, the thoughts that Clatter
In the brain that defines you,
You are your grey matter.
This is an opportunity for you to recognise.

If you have been wronged, tell it
If you have succeeded, tell it
If you have got something to say
Write it, speak it
Give your story the platform, the stage, the arena
It deserves – you deserve.
For you are a sentient being, you have a voice,
You have a platform, you have a stage,
You have an arena,
Do not let what others think dissuade
You from your own truth.
This is an opportunity for you to recognise.

When You Got The Goblin Market

You got it and I saw it in your eyes.
And I loved the way you raised your hand,
Not rushed but deliberate, as though even
That mundane gesture was to be savoured.
You raised your hand as though you were
Reaching for the sky. You looked like a
Statue crafted as a testament to triumph.
This, in contrast to the loucheness of those
Who would normally acknowledge that they
Have the answer, have all the answers, by a
Casual raising of a pen in languid fingers from
An arm attached to an elbow planted firmly
On the table. I saw you had something
To say and your precise analytical insight
Into Christina Rossetti's motivations was
A turning point from which you grew and grew.
And from that moment on you knew you
Belonged in a world of words and thoughts
And discussions and ideas.

The Retardation of a Generation

**Come and see the retardation of a generation.
Come and see schools,
react to tabloid paranoia,
and on the instruction of fools
report parents to social services
for the crime of
allowing their children
to cycle to school
or wait for a bus, on their own,
a 100 yards from their own home.
Come and watch the playground ban
on British Bulldog and football,
the result of an attempt to make
childhood anti-septic by
people who state 'you can't say
brainstorm in the classroom,
'It's offensive to epileptics'.
Those, who at first sight
of two boys having a fight
forget what it's like to be
13 and hormonal and call in a
shrink because they think that they
have to be seen to be safeguarding,
whatever that means,
when in my experience of every
punch up I had as a kid the next thing
my opponent and I did was laugh
as the teacher would make us
realise how daft we were to
be fighting. Then we would go
and join in a 17 a side game of
football, the scores standing at**

22 all that would break for lessons
about the horrors of war, and how to
bore holes in metal and wood, where it
was understood that we were responsible
for our own safety when using tools.
And science lessons where we blew things
up after mixing chemicals in cups
and English where we read
To Kill A Mockingbird and
discussed Atticus Finch and
his attempts to stop Tom Robinson
getting lynched in a book
where the use of the word nigger
didn't make us snigger because
we understood the implications of
that word due to it not being skipped
over by a teacher scared of being
censured by a form of fascism
called political correctness. If
we want this generation to learn
independence then they have
to become emotionally intelligent
and intellectually mature. And to
secure that aspiration then
politicians and OFSTED and
those 'experts' in education
need to be aware that handing out
GCSEs on a plate will seal the fate
of a retarded generation, because
there is no success in gaining 10
A stars if you don't know who
Shelley or Mozart are, or aren't
aware of the causes of the Second World War.

How can a child be called educated if
facts and figures are handed to them
shrink wrapped and plated for fear
that if left to their own devices schools
won't hit the targets set that year?
So let's tell the Elmer Gantry politicians,
who stand there like neo-con men preachers,
blaming everything on bad teachers
when they are the ones insisting on
making the youth pay for something
that was free back in their day,
lose your targets, they make no sense
as do your ridiculous attempts
to sanitise education. Because
omitting the painful
truths of the human condition
will inevitably lead to the
retardation of a generation.

Mind The Gap

Hadrian's Wall, what's that?
Please mind the gap.

Of course I've heard of Wagner, he's from X-Factor!
Please mind the gap.

Why did Orwell set 1984 in the past?
Please mind the gap.

The reason for the fall of the Berlin Wall, was it an earthquake? I don't know, it happened before I was born.
Please Mind the gap.

Nelson Mandela, he captained HMS Victory, didn't he?
Please mind the gap

Sir, Where is South Africa exactly?
Please mind the gap...
Mind the gap...
The gap...

Advice To A Teacher Doing Last Minute Cover

Maths: Ask them to work out the √ of minus 1.

English: Tell them there's a spelling test and read out words like 'particularly', extraneously and equilibrium.

Geography: Ask them to identify and classify cloud formations.

Citizenship: List all countries in the United Nations.

Chemistry: Reclassify the periodic table so that it rhymes.

History: List, not only the dates of significant events in World War II, but also the times.

Sociology: Discuss, in pairs, what are acceptable and unacceptable crimes in relationship to the post-modern paradigm.

Physics: Do a real life experiment on Schrödinger's Cat and if covering Biology then repeat that.

Media Studies: Stick a film on.

Sauberung

If the books look scruffy bin them,
We must look tidy for the inspectors.

(No thoughts of new shelves or cupboards)

Are they scruffy because they've been neglected?
Or have you considered the phrase 'well thumbed'?
How about 'well used'?
How about 'valuable academic resource'?

No? Just scruffy old books then,
Books the inspectors might object to?
Oh, well bin them then.
Or better still burn them and cry
Sauberung, Sauberung, Sauberung.

Part Five: In Memoriam

I Wasn't There

**My Great Grandad Stanley Shaw,
The Dad my Nan never saw.
You went over the top at the sound
Of the of the officers whistle and Gun
On the first day of the Somme
While your daughter was in Nanny Shaw's womb.
Did you know you had a child on the way
As you lay, dying there?**

I don't know, I wasn't there.

**Great Uncle Georgie, Nanny Ivy's brother,
When she spoke of you her eyes moisten,
Her lips quiver.
You caught Typhoid as you and your mates
Helped those living skeletons
By sharing your rations behind Belsen's gates.
You lay there dying in a field hospital bed
Surrounded by the living dead
Put there by men with skulls on their caps
And the mark of Kane forever on their backs.
How did you feel, the war nearly over, dying there?**

I don't know, I wasn't there.

**My Grandad George, you gave me your Mercury badge,
That winged god who carried messages from HQ to The front
In Tunisia and Salerno and Cassino Mount.
Where, despite the Italian surrender you and your Mates bore the brunt.
Where you gained your hidden away oak leaves of Bronze.
You told me once you fought Nazis not Germans.**

Then after showing me the scar
Where a bullet 'parted your hair',
You replaced your hand knitted wooly hat
And walked into your council house garden
To stand and stare. Were you back there?

I didn't ask, only you know that.
I wasn't there.

To A Bereaved Friend

Soak me with your tears,
Smother me with your grief,
Be a sobbing rag doll in my arms.
Cry on me,
Rage at me.
I'll listen, I won't talk;
It's your anger, your sadness,
Your confusion of thoughts.
I'll be your emotional punch bag,
Your rock of flesh and bone.
And when that storm has blown out
You can compose yourself
And be strong for those
Who lean on you.
Then, when it's right to do so
Fill that hole in your heart where he used to belong
With all the memories you have of him
And let those times carry you.

Tribute To Gil Scott-Heron

Connecting The Last Poets to Chuck D and KRS1, a poet, lyricist and jazz pianist. Sublime in his delivery, both poetically and vocally.

A 12" single heard round a mate's house whilst illicitly bunking off school, Uno, Dos, Uno, Dos Tres, Quatro; That voice, that countdown to the opening of The Bottle.

That moment so clear that I remember vowing to go to London the next Saturday and spend every penny I had on the records of Gil Scott-Heron.

And I did, and I learnt that 'Home Is Where The Hatred Is', that 'Whitey's On The Moon, and that 'The Revolution Won't Be Televised'.

Gil Scott-Heron, a genius in these blue eyes.

Ticket to Ride

**Is there something metaphorical,
or tempting the inevitable, about
getting on a bus to the hospital
and only asking for a single?**

Thank you for investing time in reading this anthology.

For more information on Jack Hughes please visit his website at
http://jackhughespoetry.webs.com/
Or email to
jackhughespoetry@yahoo.co.uk

For proof reading, editing services and creative writing courses visit The Mighty Pen at
http://mightypen.webs.com/
Or email to the.mightypen@hotmail.com

For information on private and small group academic tuition at A Level, HE Level, Study Skills courses and advice on home schooling please visit Academy Education at
http://academyeducation.webs.com/
Or email to
academyeducation2010@hotmail.co.uk

About the Author

Jack Hughes is a blogger, essayist, reviewer, poet, spoken word artist and creative writing teacher.

Jack was born at the back end of the 60s in Park Royal Hospital, Willesden to a signwriter Father and an insurance clerk Mother.

His earliest memory is cutting his head open at the age of four whilst playing in the garages at the bottom of the estate he lived on in Chesham, Bucks.

A childhood, teens and 20s growing up in Banbury, Oxfordshire gave him his lifelong friends, a desire for travel and an ability to drink.
Jack now lives in Bournemouth and lectures in an FE College. His background in mixing both plaster and mortar acting as the bedrock for his academic attainment at Bournemouth, Portsmouth and Oxford Universities.

His favourite colour is cornflower blue, favourite city is Paris, doesn't support a football team despite being urged to by the marketing dept. and has a burning ambition to learn Latin and Yiddish.

Jack Hughes is a nom de plume.

www.ingramcontent.com/pod-product-compliance
Ingram Content Group UK Ltd.
Pitfield, Milton Keynes, MK11 3LW, UK
UKHW020237250726
13967UKWH00001B/421

9 781447 766407